TEENTIN

STORIES ALL ABOUT TEENAGE

SIMRAN RANA

Copyright © Simran Rana
All Rights Reserved.

This book has been published with all efforts taken to make the material error-free after the consent of the author. However, the author and the publisher do not assume and hereby disclaim any liability to any party for any loss, damage, or disruption caused by errors or omissions, whether such errors or omissions result from negligence, accident, or any other cause.

While every effort has been made to avoid any mistake or omission, this publication is being sold on the condition and understanding that neither the author nor the publishers or printers would be liable in any manner to any person by reason of any mistake or omission in this publication or for any action taken or omitted to be taken or advice rendered or accepted on the basis of this work. For any defect in printing or binding the publishers will be liable only to replace the defective copy by another copy of this work then available.

I would love to dedicate my work to my lovely parents "Mr. Amit Rana & Mrs. Shalini Rana."

Scottish International School
Shamli

Contents

Simran Rana

I've been crafting stories since I was old enough to hold a pencil. Though I write in the clean and wholesome stories, I like heroines sassy and their struggles to be real. You'll find happy endings, yes, but a lot of mess along the way—and maybe some laughs. Just like real life.

My parents, family, teachers, principal and school have always been my pillars of strength and have always motivated me to achieve my goals.

I am thirteen years old and like any other teenager, I have also faced some problems of teenage and through this book, I have come up with some stories which contain all those problems and the bonus point is that they have the solution as well.

So go ahead and enjoy the book !

About The Book

'Teentin' is all about Teenage stories. These stories have the problems and solutions for many teenage problems. Reading these stories will be interesting and helping. You will get motivated, inspired and hopefully, this book will also act like a stress buster. The stories have entertaining characters - some will make you laugh whereas some will make you angry that why did it do this. Reading this book will help you relate your problems and you will also get solutions to all those.

Come on! Let's get started!

A Book By

PENAAKI

THE RIGHT PATH

Stress is just the fear of mind, sometimes it will try to divert you from your goal but you just keep going! Happiness and achievements will become the showstoppers!

Once there was a city called Oslao. In the city center, was a small but beautiful house. There lived a family of 4. Mom and dad had 2 children - Rosette and Rosemary. Both the sisters were teenagers and were always against each other, ready to fight but on the other hand, they both couldn't live without each other. Both of them used to go to the same school from childhood. Rosette loved her school as if it was a dream palace whereas Rosemary didn't like going to school. Rosette always scored well in her examinations but Rosemary was much interested in games rather than studies. Their mother, Mrs. Richard was a school teacher. She taught in the same school. Rosette adored the school so much that even on every non-working day, she liked to visit the school with her mother. She knew all the teachers of the school and most of all, she loved her principal. She was totally mad after her. She admired her. Everyday, whenever she used to visit the school, she went to the principal's office and talked to her. Whenever she went to her office, invariably, she had some ideas for the school's welfare and betterment. Every morning, she sent a message to her principal, "Good morning ma'am!" Rosette had even pasted her principal's photo in her room. She saved her number with the name "Adopted Mumma." Her principal also talked to her nicely and politely. This kept going but once, when

Rosette had her maths examination, she was not confident enought to write the exam properly. In the morning, she kept crying saying, "I haven't prepared anything Mom! What will I do? I am sorry.. " In this fear, Rosette did something which she wasn't meant to do. She made cheating chits and kept them in her pocket. When she was writing her exams, she didn't use them because she knew that this would be wrong so she just took them out and kept them in her desk. She wrote her exam honestly without using any unfair means but a boy, who was sitting just behind Rosette, saw those chits which she kept in her desk and started shouting, "Chits! Chits! Rosette has chits!" Rosette was very afraid. The invigilator, after seeing all this, came to Rosette and asked, "Why did you bring these chits? You know these are not allowed in the haul." A petrified Rosette lied and said, "No madam! I didn't bring these. These were already there inside my desk. I noticed them at first but then I thought why to worry about this and I left them untouched." The invigilator said, "I don't care. You should have thrown these out of your bench. Give me those chits. I will show them to your class teacher." Roseate was so terrified that she gave them to her and started crying. She didn't let anyone realise that those chits were hers but inside, she was dying of guilt. The co-ordinator - Ms. D'Souza was on round. The invigilator saw her and showed the chits to her and told her everything. Ms. D'Souza took the chits with her and went. Rosette thought that she might have ignored this but actually, she didn't. Ms. D'Souza came back and asked the invigilator for Rosette's answer sheet. The invigilator gave the sheet to Ms. D'Souza. The co-ordinator also called Rosette outside the haul. She very politely asked, "Rosette, you are a good girl. Whatever I ask you, just tell me the truth. Are these chits?" Rosette was still scared to tell the truth so she lied to her again and said, "No ma'am. These were already there inside my desk." Ms. D'Souza asked, "You are an intelligent girl. You know that no paper should be kept inside the bench. Then why did you not throw these chits away?" Rosette kept quiet. Ms. D'Souza asked again, "Are these chits yours? Please tell me the truth so that I can save you." After listening to this, Rosette told her the truth. Ms. D'Souza said, "Ok. Let us just do one thing, you give me everything in written, admiting that you had chits and I won't tell anything to anyone." Rosette gave her a slip in which everything was written clearly. Ms. D'Souza took the slip. Rosette requested, "Ma'am, please don't tell anything to anyone." Ms. D'Souza knew that Rosette was a sincere girl and won't do this again so she said, "Don't worry dear, forget what happened!" Rosette was a bit relaxed after listening this. Days passed and this also flew away from everyone's mind. Now, it was Rosette's principal's birthday. As a gift, Rosette had written letters for her principal in which she wrote how much she loved her. Her principal has her birthday on October 9 which was Sunday so Rosette gave the letters to her principal on 8th. Her principal, on seeing so many letters said, "What is this? You are busy writing these letters only. Why can't you study a bit? I know everything. I know that you cheated. You should not have done this! Will you do all this now? I already told you to focus on maths. Didn't I? It was your maths exam right? Ms. D'Souza came to me with all those chits the same day! Why did you do this? Go to tution if you are weak at maths! Study! Now go! I have a meeting." Rosette was totally heartbroken. Rosette gave a badge to her principal on which "Birthday Girl" was written. She said, "Wear this tomorrow." And left. Rosette went in the playground and started crying. She kept crying for an hour. She shouted, "Why did I do this?" No sooner, she realised she was wrong and went inside the campus. But still, for many days, Rosette did not seem to be fine. Afterall, it was the first time that the person whom she loved so much had scolded her so badly. After some days, Rosette's principal called her. She said, "Rosette, I know whatever happened was not appreciable at all. I didn't expect this from you sweetheart so I just coul not stop myself from scolding you. I know you are hurt but Rosette, just think once, do you think whatever you did was right? It was not darling. Sometimes, when we are afraid of something, we often take wrong steps that we shouldn't but what can we even do? It is a common human tendency but my dear, our job is to stop ourselves from doing such nincompoop activities. Promise me, that you won't repeat it. You will learn to control yourself." "Sorry ma'am. I know that whatever I did was wrong but because of my fear, I couldn't stop myself. I promise, I promise I will never do this again. I will study more next time. I will learn to control myself. I will improve my skills and I will become a good girl." said Rosette. To this, her principal replied, "That's like my girl. Always remember Rosette, fear will try to distract you but your job is to focus and walk on the right path!" Then Rosette said, "Ok ok I have understood but you please don't scold me like this now onwards. It hurts." Both of them then laughed out loud.

CALMNESS IS THE KEY

Be calm, be forgiving, Be you, Be strong, let this be your forte !

2

Once there was a village. On its periphery was a big house. It was an abode of a very happy family. Mom and Dad were blessed with a 13 years old son and 4 years old daughter. They chose beautiful names-Mark and Catherine. Mark was a very generous and loving brother. He was always there to tend her. He used to fulfil all her wishes. One day she expressed her will to go to nearby wood. Its trees adorned with different hued flowers caught her attention. She very sweetly hugged Mark and said, "Dear bro! I want to see what is there inside that great wood. Could you please take me there?" Mark caressed hair and said, "Why not little sis? How about visiting the wood on coming Sunday?" Catherine's eyes gleamed with happiness. "Oh! You are such an Angel to me. How blessed I feel to have a brother like you!" Now Catherine started longing for the upcoming Sunday and started preparing for it. She brought a beautiful pink coloured basket which was gifted to her by her grandmother. She put her doll, various balls and small colourful marbles into it. She went to her mother and kissed her. Now mama knew that her daughter is pampering her for getting something. She very sweetly hugged her looking into her bright eyes. Mother asked, "What do you want my child?" "Oh mom! you are a darling. You know what I want, I and brother are going to visit the wood on coming Sunday. Would you be kind enough to make some cupcakes, sandwiches and shake to carry along with us?" "Why not? Always at your disposal my dear daughter." Slowly but steadily, the long awaited Sunday arrived. There was a great-hustle-bustle in the house. Mom was busy in kitchen packing the favourite cupcakes, puddings, shakes and sandwiches. Father was busy in instructing them what to do, what not to do. They promised that they will take all care. "Wow! What a splendid wood it is brother! There are so many butterflies. Please look at your left where we find that oak tree. Can you see that beautiful bird? What do we call it? It si Elegant trogon. Just have a look at its white at pink belly. It makes it distinct. This green world is mesmerizing. I wish I could live here forever!" said Catherine and run towards a bush. She wanted to pluck carnations blooming beautifully. Ass soon as she came near the bush and plucked the flowers, a loud scream pricked Mark's heart. "What happened!" Mark ran towards that direction and shrieked which was spine nearing. He could not see his little sister covered by the swarm of bees. It was a mind numbing experience. He bellowed and bawled but in vain. After one hour the swarm left. It was really shocking for him to see pitiable and poignant situation of his sister. "Catherine! My little sis, please get up." He took her in his arms and carried her tothe carriage. It seemed like years passing to reach home. He was so mouthful that he cursed the little insects who were the cause of Catherine's pain. "Let all the bees vanish from the world. Not a single to live!" The moment he uttered these words, the fairy of wishes heard it. She knew that Mark is very docile. She moved her wand and uttered, "Abra ka Dabra. Gilli Gilli Shuh. Wishes of thos boy, Finds a way soon!" And lo! All the directions were covered by the swarms of bees. They were falling like cats and dogs. Soon there were piles of carcasses of bees. Mark saw this. He did not mean that Is my wish granted! Now it was the time to repent. He ran towards his father who had already called a doctor who was treating his soul, his little sister, who was now calm as the doctor had already smeared balm on her and injected so that the swelling can submerge. A smile faintly shore on his face. His sister was fine now. He near his father and told everything. Father scolded him for wishing such a nincompoop wish. He told it was not the fault of bees. It was his sister's fault. But now what is the use of crying over spilt milk? Mark went to his room and lighted a candle and again wished, "Let all the bees revive. Suddenly a fairy appeared. She told him, "Mark you are a good boy but always remember that never ever wish that can harm the whole creation of the lord." Mark was pale. His eyes were full of tears. He bowed down and asked the fairy, "Oh fairy mother! Please forgive me. I won't repeat it. Please reverse your boon." Fairy told him that there is a way. "On the left corner of the wood, there's a canal. You will find a group of 4 to 6 bees there. Now it is time for you to repay. Help them to multiply so that they can again enjoy this blissful creation." Mark contacted his science teacher who was an active member of National Bee Research Center who helped him in installing bee and taught him how to feed them. After one month, there were six hundred bees. Mark was happy. He also recieved an award for saving the species. Even Mark's school, appreciated and honoured him with a trophy, medal and certificate. All his friends and teachers were proud of him. Being seated with his father, Mark shout out loud, "Don't cure but reverse your anger! Your hatred.."

EMOTIONAL BUT STRONG

Pain comes, pain goes. Sadness comes, sadness goes but our job is to face everything positively.

3

Bella was a teenager. She had flat nose, a dark complexion, straight but short hair and short height. She was a bit emotional. She lived with her mother-father and two little brothers. She lost her father about a year ago. She used to stay upset after her father's death and everyone knew it. Although, she was a strong girl but still a death shattered her all. She always uploaded sad status, sad photos. Initially, everyone took care of her but later some people started taking advantage of her. They used to tease her by saying, "Bella is a cry baby! Bella is a cry baby!" She used to stay very sad because of this. Sometimes she even cried sitting in the corners but some months later, her pain and sadness changed into irritation. She started fighting with everyone and especially with one of her friends, Anita. She faught with her every single time on smallest to biggest issues. Also, she started hating her mother, she said, "Neither I value my mother nor she values me." Once, Bella started to fight with Anita on a petty issue. She said, "Anita you are such an idiot! Do you even know anything? I don't know from where such people come from!" Anita felt really bad, she didn't say anything and ran away crying. Anita was very emotional and sensitive. She was very sweet and helping but she didn't know what to do in reaction to Bella's words. She complained to the teachers about Bella's behaviour but none of the teacher would help her. They only said, "Anita, you are an intelligent girl. You know Bella lost her father some months ago, she is depressed and emotionally weak. We have to be with her not punish her! Try to understand dear." No-one would help Anita so she thought of handling the issue herself. She tried to talk to Bella. She thought that if she would understand how Bella actually feels then maybe she would be able to help her and she would stop fighting so one day, she went to Bella and said, "Bella, I know you miss your father but you need to understand that the way you talk, the way you behave is not appreciable. No-one likes the way you talk." Bella was also a good girl, it was just that she wasn't able to let her anger, pain and sadness out which was reflecting in hr personality now-a-days. Bella said, "I am sorry Anita for whatever I have said and whatever I have done. I really miss my father." Slowly, Bella started sharing her things with Anita. Anita also tried to help her as much as she could. Gradually, their relations improved and they became best friends. Bella also improved herself. She tried not to shout and notto be very annoying. Anita asked Bella to write poems in which she could let her feelings out and Bella did the same. Bella wrote poems and lo! Her poems became so famous that she launched a book full of poems. Anita also wrote stories so she also got a book published of her own. Both of them were now budding authors and best friends!

THE STORY OF FREE TAXI SERVICE

When you have the right dreams, right intentions and dedication, even God supports you!

4

Naira was a 13 year old girl. She was very sweet and helping. She wanted to have a bicycle so that she could learn how to ride it. She always used to tell her mom that, "Mumma, first I will learn to ride a bicycle, then motorbike and then later on I will start free taxi services for the needy people who can not pay the rents but have to go to different places." She lived in a joint family in a two story house. They also had a tenant who lived on the first floor. The tenant was a banker. He lived alone. He was very nice and polite. He did not speak much. He had his wife and a son as the family but they lived in Kangra, his hometown. The tenant was named Karan Sharma. He originally hailed from Himachal Pradesh but due to his posting in Shamli, he had to live at Naira's house as a tenant. Every Saturday, he went to Kangara to visit his family. He used to come back on Monday mornings. He returned to Naira's house in the evening. There were two doors at Naira's house – one main gate which gave the entry in the porch and a door which was the entrance to the house. The house members had to open both gates for Karan's entrance – one for Karan and one for his bike. One evening, when Karan was back home, it was Naira who was there to open the doors for him. Firstly, she opened the door which was the entrance to the house, and then she opened the main gate for entering the porch. When Karan parked his bike in the porch, Naira was trying to close the gate but was failing to do so as the gate was huge and heavy. After seeing this, Karan said, "It's alright Naira, I'll close it. You can go." Naira went into the room after this. But the problem here was that the lock of the gate was inside but Karan had to go outside to enter from the house door so he just closed the gate and didn't lock it. At 11:00 p.m., when Naira and all other family members were sitting and talking, her mother noticed that the key of Naira's bicycle which her father had bought today was not there on the key holder so she went in the porch to check whether the key was lying there or not, as soon as she reached in the porch, she was shocked to see that Naira's bicycle was missing and the gate was also opened. She screamed, "Rahul(Naira's father)!" as it was a surprise for Naira. In no time, Rahul arrived in the porch. Rahul asked – "Anjali, who opened the gate when Karan came?" Anjali replied – "Naira." So Rahul called Naira and asked – "Naira, did you lock the gate after Karan parked his bike?" Naira said – "No Daddy. I was unable to close the gate so Karan uncle said that he would lock it." Rahul was certain that Karan could not lock the gate or probably he forgot to do so he thought of asking him what really happened. He shouted – "Karan!" Karan and other family members also reached the porch and asked – "What's the matter Rahul? Why are you shouting?" Rahul said – "I had bought a bicycle for Naira as a surprise and now it's not here. I am sure that Karan couldn't lock the gate so I wanted to ask him whether he locked it or not?" To this Karan replied – "Rahul, I was supposed to come from the house door and I had to go outside to reach the door. Therefore, I just closed the gate and came." After listening this all the members were upset and thought that the bicycle has been robbed. Everyone went into the room thinking that there is no use sitting and waiting for the bicycle to come here. While Naira's family was wondering about the cycle, Naira started to cry and said, "I wanted a bicycle, daddy bought it for me. I want it back..." Rahul saw this and after listening to Naira, Rahul called someone. After thirty minutes, Anjali screamed, "Naira! Come to the porch!" In a minute, Naira arrived there and everyone started singing the Happy Birthday song. The bicycle was also parked in the porch. It was a brand new bicycle. It was of black colour - Naira's favourite colour. It seemed to b expensive. Naira was ecstatic to see all this and started to tear up. Naira asked,"Daddy, was this your plan?" To this Rahul answered,"Yes my princess, I thought why not surprise you in a different way? Now you're a step forward for your dream Free Taxi services." Then, Naira's mother said, "Naira, my sweetheart, my darling, always remember, when you have a good intention, everyone is with you, even God is with you!"

THE CREATIVE MIND

Creativity in mind, Pen in hands, a paper in front. This is world!

5

William was a 13 years old boy. He had curly-noodle-like hair, round face, kind heart and a very creative mind. William lived with his mother, Margaret. Margaret was a single parent. William's father died a few years ago and after his death, Margaret was thrown out of the house as Margaret's in-laws had a very poor mentality. They believed that the reason their son died was Margaret. Margaret was an orphan. Hence, she didn't have any place where she could stay so in the early days, she stayed at one of her friends house and later she opened a small café which was running well. William went to a small school where children were only supposed to score well whereas William was totally a different guy. He was much more interested in painting rather than studies so he didn't use to score well in his examinations. He had a great talent, whatever came to his mind, he used to draw it. All the portrais that he made were just like real people. We can say that he was a god gifted child. His mother knew everything that he had amazing painting and writing skills but because she wasn't very strong financially, she couldn't send her child to a good school where her child could be given the wings to fly in his own kind of sky. Margaret was regularly searching for a good trainer when one day, William came home crying and sobbing. Margaret asked him, "What happened my child?

Is everything ok? Why are you crying?" "Mumma, I got scolded by my teacher today, so badly.. I couldn't score well mumma! What will happen of me? Will I become a dumb? Will I always be called a failure? Oh mummy, I can't understand anything!" said William. Margaret felt really bad after she saw and listen all this. She motivated him and said, "Oh darling.. don't worry! Your marks don't decide your future or your personality. I know you are a wonderful painter! You make so beautiful paintings. You can build a bright future in this field my dear! Mom will help you! I am always with you my son!" William was quite relieved now but still some questions in his mind were disturbing him repeatedly - "How will I improve my skills? How will I show my talent to the world?" One fine day, he took some of his paintings to school and pasted them on his class's soft board. That day, randomly, the new principal of his school came in his class. She noticed the paintings of William and she asked, "Who has made these paintings?" All the children in the class started taking the name of William. They all thought that the principal would punish William for the paintings as the ex-principal didn't allow paintings in the school. A terrified William stood up and said, "I have made these madam." The principal looked at William and said, "Wow! I have never seen such realistic and beautiful paintings. You made my day! What is your name?" "Thank you ma'am! My name is William, William Stanford." said William. The principal was a nice and loving lady. She had a great teaching experience of about 26 years. She had as the principal of many schools. She knew 5 languages which made her a linguist. Her belief was, "Every child is a beautiful flower, a flower that has its own colour, a flower that has its own fragrance and teachers must nurture the uniqueness." She took William in her office and asked him,

"Hi William! How are you doing?" To this, William answered, "Good morning ma'am! I am fine!" Then, the principal asked him about his hobbies and interests. She said, "What are your hobbies? I was looking at your report card and I didn't find a good score so are you interested in something else? You make such nice paintings, are you interested in painting?" "Yes ma'am. You guessed it right. I have been painting and making portraits for a few years now. I want to become a painter, an artist but I am afraid, I don't know how to show my talent to people! Will you help me ma'am?" said William. The principal replied, "That's awesome William! Definately I will help you out but tell me, what kind of paintings do you make? And also, I have never seen your portraits. Could you show some of them?" William answered, "Of course ma'am, I will show you the portraits. Ma'am, I basically like to paint sceneries, object drawings and all that kind of stuff." The principal was happy to acknowledge this. She said, "Brilliant! Ok so firstly, tomorrow, you show me the portraits then, woh go to your arts teacher and ask her if you have to improve somewhere. Daily, you got to her in your free lesson and learn from her. But for now, start uploading the pictures of your paintings and portraits on social media. This will make people aware of you. Later, you can tie up with some e-shopping site and start selling your paintings there. Then you can take part in competitions and stuff like that. And remember William, I am always with you. Whenever you need help, I am there." William was very happy to see this. He had finally got an answer to his questions. His principal continued to help him and in improving his skills. Margaret was also ecstatic after seeing her son's progress. Slowly, William became a renowned artist. He became the youngest author of his district. Days passed and William continued to touch greater heights. People like William's principal are much required in the society who can help children achieve their goals and identify the talent, the people who can enrich the personalities of all those youngsters who feel left out in twenty first century's crowd.

REALIZATION

Influence yourself in the right manner, don't let others influence you in the bad manner.

6

Long ago, one day, there lived a young girl named Swarna. She was 13 years old. She lived with her father - Pankaj. Pankaj was a single parent. Julie's mother died just after her delivery. Swarna wasn't a good mixer. She didn't like socializing. She neither had any friends to whom she could talk nor she chatted with any relatives. Even she didn't like to share everything with her father. Her father, Pankaj, was a busy man. He left home in the morning and returned back at night so even Swarna didn't get a chance to talk to him. Swarna also got influenced very easily which is quite normal as a teenager. Although, a little bit of guidance could improve this but in Swarna's case, there was no one who could help her out as she didn't have anyone with whom she could share her things. Once, while returning back to home, she saw a group of street girls who were wandering around the streets. Her heart knew that they were wrong but somewhere she was attracted towards them. She went to them and asked, "Hi! Who are you?" To this one of the girls from the gang replied, "Hey you moron! Are you even talking to us? We are the great Gangi bangi of this area!" Julie was a bit afraid after listening to this but still she asked, "Can I join you?" The gang was shocked to see this. The same girl said, "Ok but you'll have to do whatever we say." Swarna agreed and now, she was also a part of the Gangi bangi gang. Her father was not known to this. Swarna used to come back before he reached home. This series kept going. Gradually, Swarna got addicted to bad habits. She wasn't interested in studies anymore. She started to fail in her examinations. Moreover, she was not interested in any hobby as well. She just wanted her mobile phone and that gang to be around. John was shocked to acknowledge all this. He knew a hard-working shy Swarna who didn't care about others but now his daughter was completely changed. This kept going but one day something very awful happened. One of the girls of the Gangi bangi gang asked Swarna to steal a silver statue of a deity which was kept in the garden of an old lady. Inside, Swarna knew that this would be wrong but the gang's influence got over her ordinations. So she went inside the garden barefoot so that there would be no sound of walking Swarna was very afraid so she kept on chanting, "Om bhoor bhuwah swah tat sa vitur varenyam bhargo devasya dhi mahi dhiyo yo na prachodayat.." The old lady was sleeping when Swarna entered the garden. Swarna kept walking slowly on the grass but she didn't see that there was a small pot which was kept along the boundary. Swarna was so terrified that she was continuously seeing the old lady sonthat she could run away if she wakes up. A scared Swarna, couldn't notice the flower pot and accidentally hit her left leg's little finger in the pot. She couldn't bear the pain and she screamed, "Oh God!" The old lady woke up as soon as she listened the scream. Swarna was crying in pain and she couldn't walk as her finger was paining like hell. Therefore, she couldn't run away as well. The lady walked to Swarna and helped her. After Swarna got some relief in her finger, the old lady asked her, "Dear, what were you doing in my garden?" Swarna was a bit afraid to tell the truth but this time she had gathered enough courage to be above-board. She said, "Aunt, I was here to steal your silver diety statue. I am sorry, I was forced to do so. I won't repeat it again? Please forgive me. Please.." The old lady knew that Swarna is a generous girl, the only problem is the bad influence and no guidance. The old lady was very sweet and helping and moreover, she knew everything about Swarna so she didn't scold Swarna instead she caressed her hair and said, "Sweetheart, I know that you didn't want to do it but due to reasons you did. Don't worry, I won't tell anything to anyone but you promise me that you will abandon that gang and whenever you want someone to be around you, without hesitation, you can come to me. Just think that I am your grandmother." Swarna was very happy to listen this. At last the old said, "Dear, always remember one thing, never let others to influence your good thoughts."

FOLLOW YOUR INTERESTS

Follow your interests, your passion, not of others!

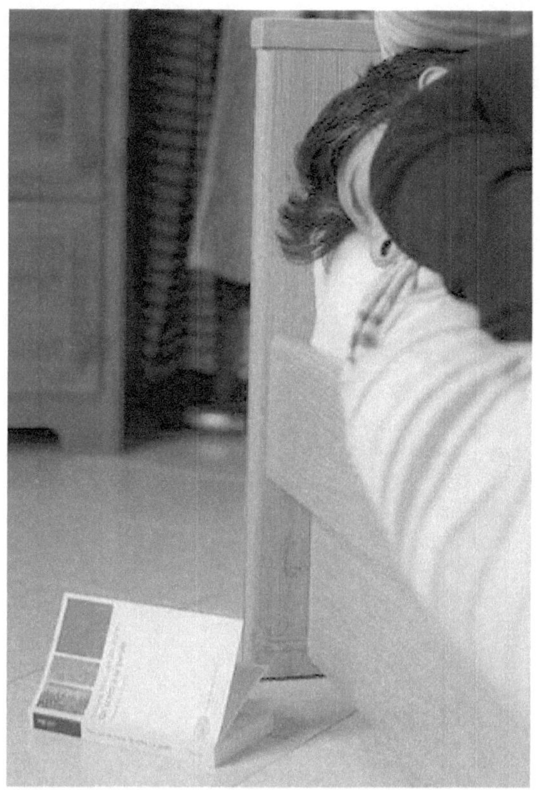

7

Nihal is a teenager but not a fresh one that means, he is a teenager but he is 16 years old. He studies in class 11th. His teachers and parents are very supportive, understanding and friendly. In 11th, Nihal has chosen Commerce as his stream. At the time of choosing the stream, Nihal was a bit under pressure. Not because of his parents' or teachers' stubbornness to choose Commerce but because of his friends. Nihal had thought to choose Humanities as he was very interested in History. He likes to gather ancient things. He has a whole collection of old things. Moreover, his love for geography and economics was unconditional. He was also good at English and Hindi and his parents and teachers were also very happy as they knew that when we follow our passion, our interests, we definately tend to something big, but Nihal's friends were not of the same kind. All of his friends were choosing Commerce as they thought that taking Commerce would result in bright future. They didn't have any interest in the subjects of Commerce but it was just a superstition which was set in their minds that choosing Commerce would make them a big man. Therefore, they started teasing Nihal by saying, "Hey! Only losers take Humanities! Hahaha!" Nihal was very upset as he couldn't understand what to do. Although, Nihal was a smart boy but still he wasn't able to identify that his friends were not worthy of being his friends. Real friends are those who help and support us not those who try to pull us back. But if we notice everyone's point of view then Nihal's friends were also not wrong, it was just the superstition that was wrong but what could be done, there was none who could explain the correct thing to them. At that time, Nihal didn't tell anything to his parents. He was confused about which stream to choose. Everytime, he just usednto ask himself, "What should I take? Humanities or Commerce? Humanities or Commerce???? What should I do?" Nihal's friends had brainwashed his mind so much that even Nihal started to think the same. Finally, the day came when all the students had to choose their streams. Nihal chose Commerce. He was mistaken here. Nihal should not have chosen Commerce as he didn't have any interest in it but because of the pressure, he took it. Days passed and now, it is almost 3 months that Nihal has chosen Commerce. Nihal now, is not as active, engaging and creative now as he was earlier. He used to be stressed about his academics. He isn't able to understand anything that the teachers are explaining him. His condition now is miserable. He cries sitting in the corner and regretting that why did he choose Commerce. One day, Nihal went to his mother, he said, "Mom, I want to have some talks with you." Nihal's mother said, "Yes Nihal. What happened? What's the matter?" Nihal told everything to his mother and he added, "Mom, I am not able to understand anything. What should I do? Neither I am able to solve any sums nor I'm able to concentrate. What should I do??" Nihal's mother had understood everything. Even she noticing Nihal from a long time so she said, "Nihal, it's okay. It happens, but baby, you must have talked to me or your father in the beginning only. Why did you not tell this to us earlier? If you would have told us then all this wouldn't have happened. Your time would have been saved." "I am sorry mom. I couldn't understand what to do. I was stressed. I am really sorry but what's the solution to this now? Will I fail? What will happen of me? What will happen of my career?" Nihal's mother could see how tensed Nihal was so she thought of motivating and encouraging him first and also she told him the solution, she said, "Nihal. Don't worry honey. It is okay. You know what, don't you remember, you can change your stream! Remember Anushka Sree? She studied in Scottish International School in Shamli. She also changed her stream in middle of the session and she topped the district! She was the DISTRICT TOPPER OF SHAMLI in Humanities. Dear, if you have interest, dedication, determination and passion, you can do anything! Now, you go, let me have a talk with your teacher." Nihal was very motivated and inspired now. The next day, in his school, his co-ordinator - Ms. Gaur saw him. She called him, "Nihal! Come here!" Nihal went to her and said, "Good morning ma'am!" Ms. Gaur said, "Nihal, your mother told me everything. Dear, you can change your stream. You just pursue your dreams Nihal. Which stream do you want to take?" Nihal answered, "Ma'am I want to take Humanities." Ms. Gaur said, "That's great! But one thing, always remember, your parents and teachers are your true mentors, whenever you feel that you need someone to help you or guide you, you can always contact us." Then she said, "All the Best Nihal! I want to remind you that there's nothing to stop you except you. This year, go for it! Go for those goals, those plans, and those trips."

ASKING FOR HELP IS STRENGTH!

Take help, be strong! No one can stop you if your intentions are true and determination is there!

8

Shariya was a young girl. She has straight hair, round face, deep eyes and chubby cheeks. She was just like an angel, sweet and beautiful. She loved to dress up everytime and shared everything with her mother. She had decorated her room like heaven. Shariya loved to listen old songs. She liked to do everything - singing, dancing, speaking, cooking, painting and what not, she was interested in everything. She used to score really well in her examinations. Her dream was to become the All India Topper in class X. She loved her family, especially her parents and school the most. She was punctual to school. She used to say, "There is some fragrance in the soil of my school. My school is my second home. I can I live there forever." Everyday, when she went to her school, she used to dress up like a very sincere but a fashionable girl. She loved to look gorgeous. Her language skills were also amazing but Shariya was not just a girly girl. She used to become a devil whenever required. All the students of her class knew that if they would do anything wrong, she would immediately tell the teacher and they would get a nice punishment. Her class's students were so scared of her that if she pot her bag on any bench, within 5 minutes, the students who would be sitting on it, would abandon it. She was an admirable girl. She was a great anchor, in all her school events, she used to do the anchoring. She was also very particular about the rules and regulations. Once, she saw a boy littering in the campus. She was very angry to see this. She said, "Hey you! Would you pick up the wrappers that someone else threw?" The boy said, "Are you mad? Why would I pick up?" Shariya said, "Then how can you think that someone else would do it? The sweepers, the aayas, the peons are also human beings. When you can't do such tasks then don't ask other people to do it. Pick all those wrappers that you threw. Now!" The boy understood Shariya's emotions for the people and picked up all the wrappers and promised, "Now I will never throw any wrapper here and there." Shariya always helped everyone. She was not at all partial. She never discriminated against anyone of the basis of their colour, caste or gender. She always supported the truth. She was one of those who could raise voice against wrong. Once, she noticed that a few boys of her class were continuously staring her. Initially, she ignored them but the whole day, situtuation didn't change. Shariya told her mother about this but her mother said, "What can we even do? They are just glancing." To this Shariya replied, "No mom. I am not feeling comfortable like this. I will have to do something." "Ok darling. Mumma is with you. Whatever you do, I am there as your pillar of support." Days passed but the boys didn't stop. Raksha Bandhan arrived. The day before Raksha Bandhan, Shariya purchased a few rakhis. She thought that if she would tie Rakhi to them, maybe they would stop. So, the next day, Shariya took rakhis to school. In the lunch break, she took out rakhis from her bag went to the boys. Firstly, they tried to run away but later a few other boys hold them tight and Shariya tied the rakhi to them. On seeing this, the class started hooting and shouting and on listening so much noice, Shariya's co-ordinator went to their classroom and asked, "Was this the class who was yelling and hooting?" Shariya said, "Yes sir." Then, the co-ordinator said, "Just tell me who were the people who were shouting. I would leave all others and punish them but if you don't tell me the names, whole class will be punished." The children didn't take any names so the co-ordinator said, "Okay. So you won't tell me the names. Fine, now get ready for the punishment. Make a queue outside the classroom." Everyone assembled outside in a line and said, "What we have to do now sir?" The co-ordinator said, "Be patient! Let me tell you. Raise your hands and take a round of the floor." Everyone was scared, especially Shariya. Although, Shariya knew that it wasn't her fault but still she was assuming that whatever is happening is because of her. The whole class took a round and went back to their class. Then, as Shariya was thinking that the ultimate fault was hers so she wrote an application pleading pardon for whatever she had done. In it, she also wrote the reason why she did it. Shariya, after writing the application, went to the co-ordinator and said, "Sir, sorry. It was me who did it all. Please forgive me but please read this application." The co-ordinator sent Shariya back to her class and read the application. Now, that he knew that the boys were disturbing Shariya. Firstly, the co-ordinator punished and made the boys understand that how disgusting it is to do such activities. The boys also apologized and promised that they would not repeat this again. Then, the co-ordinator called Shariya and said, "Shariya, always remember, there is a solution to every problem. I knew you are brave enough to handle such people but dear, always and always share your problems with your teachers and parents. See, now that you shared everything with me, I took out a solution but if you would not have done this so maybe the situation would have become worse. And yes, I salute your courage that you handled this with so much patience. I appreciate it!"

LOVE OR OVERATTACHMENT?

Love people, Care for people but never get overattached because one sided attachment kills.

9

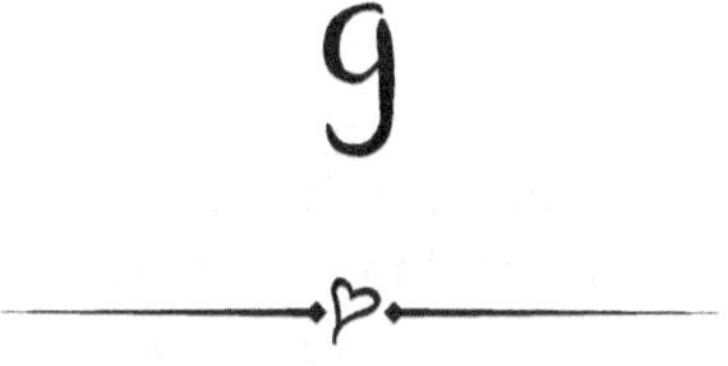

Carla was a gorgeous teenager. She was the only chid to her mom and dad. Mom and dad prayed a lot for the birth of Carla and the results of their prayer were meticulous. The family lived on the Atlantic outposts of Spain. They originally hailed from UK but due to some reasons, they were residing in Spain. Carla was an all rounder. She was a role model for all other children. Carla was also very fond of nature, plants, animals, and especially birds. Carla's dad was a renowned farmer. He had acres of land. In one of his most huge lands, he had grown trees, variety of trees, he had grown almost all the varieties which were found in Spain. This land was very close their house, it was just a few steps away. Everyday, after coming back from school, Carla spent atleast an hour there. It was the most lovable place for Carla. She always said, "This place is so wonderful! The greenery is so refreshing! The woods make me feel like I am a forest fairy. The fragrance of the small flowers grown on-thier-own is just so good and the fresh oxygen purifies my my heart and soul." One day, Carla went to her mother and said, "Oh mom! You are so sweet! You are so loving and caring! What can I do for you? Do you need any help?" Carla's mom understood that there was something that Carla wanted so she said, "Oh my god! What has happened to you today? So changed! Now don't beat around the bush and tell me what do you want?" Carla said, "Ok.. so now that you know, Mommy, my dearest, loveliest mommy, can we please go to that land where there are a lot trees, where I go daily for camping? Please.." "Oh so that's the matter! But when are you planning for this?" asked mom. Carla replied, "Oh mom, I was thinking for this Sunday. Can we please?" "Oh Calra! Don't you remember that your dad has an important meeting in the other city on Sunday with his clients? How can we got then?" answered mom. To this Carla said, "It is okay mom! You and I can go there alone. It is not so far. Come on momma!" Carla forced her mom so much that her mom had to say, "Ok ok, we will go. Happy now?" To this Carla said, "Oh mom, You are such a darling! You are such an Angel to me! So mom, now that we are going, can you also make some cupcakes, sandwiches and shakes for the day?" Her mother said, "Now that we are going... Of course sweetheart! I will make whatever you say." Carla was now eagerly waiting for the day to come. Finally the day arrived and there was a hustle in the house. Her mother was busy packing delicious cupcakes, mouth-watering sandwiches and thich smooth shakes. Whereas, Carla was busy packing the tent and a few other things necessary for camping. Although, the land was a bit small for camping but still Carla wanted to do it. As soon as they packed everything, Carla's mother took the car keys, went to the car, sat inside and said, "All set to go!" They were doing it just like they would have done if it would be a proper camping area. Carla was very happy. In no time, they reached their destination, mom and Carla took all the bags out and started assembling the camp. At first, they failed to do so but later, after reading the manual and trying numerous times, they succeeded. Then, both of them went jogging. They were damn tired after all this so after some time, they ate all the snacks that mom had prepared. Later, in the afternoon, mom said, "Carla, I am very exhausted now. I want to take a nap. You have fun but don't go too far. Mommy loves you sweetheart!" and went to sleep in the tent. Carla thought, "Why not I go and see all the trees? Let me see if any insects or birds are there.." Keeping the same in mind, Carla went to see the trees. After she walked a bit, she noticed a canary laying on the ground. She took in her hands and said, "What has happened to you? Let me see." So she rotated it and saw that one of its wings was broken. She immediately took her to her tent and started to find out the first aid box. She gave the bird first aid and fed it some water and seeds that they had. In some time, her mom also woke up. She saw the canary in Carla's hands so she asked, "Why is this canary in your hands Carla?" Carla told her mom everything and also told her about the first aid that she gave. After listening to Carla, her mother said, "I am proud of you Carla. You have saved a life today!" Carla was happy to listen this so she said, "Thank you mumma! Mumma, I was thinking why not take the canary home? I will be able to take care of her nicely then." Mom said, "Umm.. okay. You can take the canary home but as soon as she gets healed, you promise me, you will let the canary go." "Yes I promise!" said Carla. "So without wasting much time, let us go to get the required stuff for canary. Shall we?" asked mom. "Yeah!!!! Let's go." Mom and Carla went to the bird market ad got all the required equipments such a cage, seeds, water pot etc. Carla started taking care of canary. After some days, Carla named canary 'Tara'. Carla took care of Tara as her own baby. She used to talk to her, fed her on time and did all the things in the best manner. Days passed and Carla got really attached to Tara and finally the day came when Tara became a healthy bird. Seeing Tara healed, mom said, "Carla, now you should let Tara fly away. Let's do it dear." As soon as this hit Carla's ears, Carla ran away. Her mother couldn't understand what actually did it mean. She was confused whether she ran to bring Tara or she didn't want to let Tara fly away so she went to Calra and asked, "Baby, why did you run away? Do you not want to let Tara go?" "No Mommy! I don't want to let Tara fly away! She is my best friend! I share everything with her. Do you know, even she talks to me! She told me about her journey. She also told me about her previous birth. I can not let her go. She is my angel." answered Carla. Mom was shocked to listen this so she said, "Carla this is not possible baby! How can a canary tell you about its previous birth? Even humans can not remember such ancient incidents! This is not possible!!! Try to understand darling. You are just too attached to Tara." Carla was not satisfied. She started to cry, took Tara and went away. Days passed and Carla's attachment towards Tara got even more awful. She was so attached to her that she didn't do anything without her. She ate with her, slept with her, talked to her and she took her everywhere where she went. Now, it was Clara's birthday and mom-dad had organised a grand birthday party. They had invited the whole society. In the party, there was a group of naughty children too. When everyone was busy in cutting the cake and dancing, celebrating, they saw the chance an went to Clara's room. There, they saw Tara. They went near it and started teasing it. They kept touching Tara's body. Tara was very annoyed. It started chirping but in the noice of music, no-one could listen it. After some time, the party got over and it was the time to give the return gifts but still the naughty children were annoying Tara. Mom came to Clara's room to take the return gifts and one of the children saw her coming. In the hustle, one of them opened Tara's cage and ran away.

Unfortunately, one of the windows of Clara's room was opened. Tara flew out. When mom came in, she couldn't find Tara in the cage so she started looking here and there but was unable to find it. Later, she saw the opened window. She understood that Tara had flown out. She took the return gifts and left. She didn't tell anyone about this because she knew that if Clara will come to know about this then she will be very upset. No-one could imagine Clara's reaction to this. After some time, when everyone left, Clara came back to her room but when she didn't find Tara there, she started screaming, "Where is Tara? Mom! Dad! Where is Tara???" Mom told everything to Clara. Clara cried a lot after listening to whatever happened. She was upset for many days but later, on her own, she forgot everything and moved on. Some days later, mom said to Clara, "Darling, I know how much you loved Tara but Claraz always remember, love and overattachment are totally two different things. When you get overattached to anyone, no matter it is a human, animal or bird, you only regret."

ARE MY PARENTS MY ENEMIES?

Your parents are your true guides, true mentors, you can't trust anyone so easily as you can trust your parents!

10

Noah was a young and handsome boy. He was 13 thirteen years old a fresh teenager. Noah was an obedient and sincere child but now-a-days he was acting weird. He was doing things which he had never done before. Noah was a kind of child who even asked his parents for his clothes. He did everything after asking to his mom-dad. Before taking part in any competitions, wearing clothes, going somewhere, he asked his parents but now he was doing the opposite. He got irritated and annoyed very easily. His screen time was also increased. Noah's mother was noticing an increase in Noah's screen time so she went to Noah and asked him toh keep down the tab after every hour. Noah had also started wearing disgusting clothes, the ones who didn't suit a good boy. He started loving wearing open shirts without wearing anything inside. His parents tried to make him understand that these weren't the symbols of sophistication but Noah didn't listen to them even once. One day, Noah's mom came to him asked, "Darling, what do you want to have today as lunch?" Noah was sitting and was busy in his tab. He was playing a video game. As soon as his mom asked him this, he said, "What mom? Make whatever you want to? Why do you have to disturb me everytime?" and left. Mom was upset to listen this. She was thinking in her mind, "Noah has changed . He wasn't like this before.

Maybe I should wait for some time. If he changes, then fine but if he doesn't then I will talk to him." Later in the evening, Noah's dad went to call him for the dinner. He said, "Noah! Come on, leave your tab now. Dinner is ready. Come and have dinner with us." Noah said, "What's the problem? Whenever I am doing something, you come to disturb me. Is it necessary to have the dinner now only? It is just 8p.m.!" Noah's dad was shocked to see Noah's behaviour. He said, "Noah! You can not talk like this. We are your parents, not your enemies! Come and have dinner or else you won't get it." Noah threw the tab on the bed, hit his leg on the door to open it and came out. He took his plate from the dining table and again went inside. Mom-dad couldn't understand what actually was going on. Noah was thinking, "I want to get rid of these people now! They keep on interrupting me. Whatever I do, they don't like it. Why don't they understand that it's my life. Why can't they just let me be who I am? They are my true enemies!" Days passed but Noah wouldn't act mature. He got even worse. One fine evening, Noah's aunt came to their residence. She had thought to spend a few days there. Her name was Brittany. Brittany, when reached their home, said, "Noah... Could you open the door please? I am here sweetheart!" Noah's aunt didn't know about Noah's increasing behaviourial issues. Noah didn't respond to his aunt's call so Noah's mother went to open the door. She said, "Oh sis! You've finally arrived!" Noah's mother was the sister of Brittany so she said, "Oh! Long time no see dear sis! How are you?" Noah's mother replied, "I am perfectly fine. Come inside please!" Brittany went inside and asked about Noah, she said, "Where is Noah sis? Is he fine?" Noah's mother started crying. She was not able to handle Noah. His behaviour with his parents were getting worse. He didn't talk to them nicely nor he answered thier questions properly. If they asked him about where he was, he used to say, "Why do you care?" Although Noah's mother was quite strong but seeing her child this way, she also became weak. She was not able to understand what to do. Noah's mother told everything to Brittany. Brittany was also astounded to listen about Noah. She first told Noah's mother that this often happens at teenage but still we have to explain Noah that how unfair this is. She asked, "Did you try to understand why Noah has been behaving like this?" "Brittany, we have asked him numerous times if there is any problem or if he thinks he needs something and he is not getting that but he doesn't answer. We have tried everything. We have explained him politely and harshly both but he doesn't understand our point, our opinion. He is not understanding that we are his parents, not his enemies. He thinks that we are the ones who try to stop him everytime he wants to do something but it's not the case. You only tell me Brittany, if your child will be playing video games all the time then won't you stop him from doing so? If he won't study at all then won't to ask him to study a bit? Tell me!" said Noah's mother. Brittany could understand her situation so she said, "I have an idea!" Noah's mother asked, "What idea? Tell me." "See, the main reason why Noah is behaving like this is that he thinks that you interrupt him in all the things right?" asked Brittany. "Right!" answered Noah's mother. "So let's not do that!" said Brittany. Listening this, Noah's mother couldn't identify what she was trying to say so she asked, "What do you mean?" Brittany answered, "Let Noah do what he wants to. If he wants to see mobile, let him. If he doesn't want to study, let him. Whatever he wants to do, you just let him. Let us see what all will he do and what all will he learn." Noah's mother agreed and told Noah's father also not to speak to Noah. Initially, Noah could not understand what actually was happening so he just ignored but days passed, and he realised that no-one was calling him for meals, no-one was coming to wake him up, no-one was talking to him and most importantly, his aunt, who was always busy in talking to him was not even giving him a look. He realised how wrong he was and how awful it was to not being talked to so he went toh his mother, father and aunt and said, "I am really sorry. I apologise from the depth of my heart. The fault was mine. I have realised my mistake. Please forgive me." Mom-dad and Brittany first kept quiet but then they said, "So now that you have realised your mistake, we forgive you but you have two promise us two things." "What two things?" asked Noah. "First, you will never repeat this and second, you will always remember that your parents are your true guides, true mentors and best friends not your enemies!" said mom-dad and Brittany. Noah agreed and they all lived happily ever after.

www.ingramcontent.com/pod-product-compliance
Lightning Source LLC
Chambersburg PA
CBHW022101150726
47990CB00003B/1187